At the Shopping Mall

Written by Margaret MacDonald

Picture Dictionary

bookshop

car park

escalator

Read the picture dictionary. You will find these words in the book.

food court

toyshop

We go to the mall.
Mum parks the car
in the car park.

directions
SHOPS
FOOD COURT
smile &
laugh
parking space

We go into the mall.
We see the escalator.
We go up
on the escalator.

light
handrail

We go to the toyshop.
The toyshop is upstairs.
We look at the toys.

things to play with
things to ride on

We see the bookshop.
The bookshop
is upstairs, too.
We go in.

magazine
book

We go down
on the escalator.
We go to
the shoe shop.

ssistance?
TICKET
advertisement
moving step

Then we go
to the food court.
The food court
is by the shoe shop.

mug
sushi

Activity Page

1. Draw the shop you like best at the shopping mall.

2. Write these sentences:

   We go to the _____ shop.

   The _____ shop is ___________.

   (upstairs/downstairs)

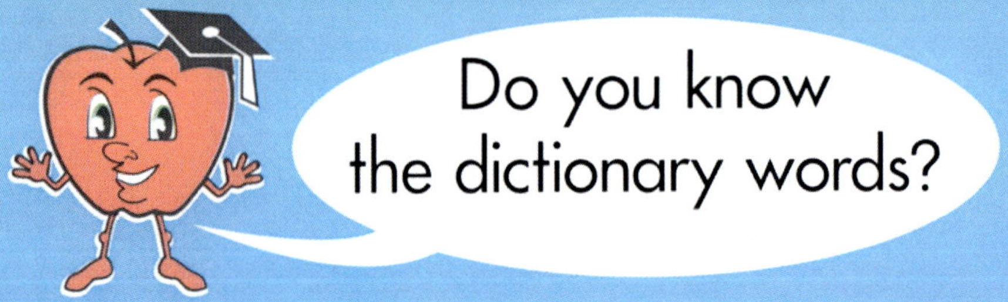